My Time, My Way

My Time, My Way

SIDNEY TUCK

StoryTerrace

Text Julie Abrams-Humphries, on behalf of StoryTerrace

Design StoryTerrace

Copyright © Sidney Tuck

Text is private and confidential

First print November 2020

StoryTerrace

www.StoryTerrace.com

CONTENTS

PREFACE

"We all have our time machines, don't we? Those that take us back are memories... And those that carry us forward, are dreams."

— *H.G. Wells*

was inspired to write this book because of my mother, who had a remarkably interesting life. She said, "If I could afford it, I would write a book about my life."

My mother lived to be over a hundred years old, and she never got around to writing that book. Reaching ninety-five myself, I thought it was about time I wrote my own life story. I have a long-standing interest in genealogy. Researching my family history has shown me that we all have a story to tell, and it is usually our own. I have been looking into our family history for over twenty years, pre-internet, discovering cousins in Australia and Canada and I even met up with one, so I wanted to condense some of my own personal history to pass on to future branches of our family tree.

In my research, I discovered a family line that dates back to the 1600s, originally from Suffolk on my father's side, including a prominent member in the eighteenth century who was blessed with longevity. He had a farm at Amwell, through which he had connections with the New River Company, he also had a number of other properties, and two inns in Hoddesdon which still exist, but with no family connection. He left some of the properties to his eldest son, provided he accepted the honorary job of workhouse master, in a long and complicated will that was difficult to read. I hope that my own history proves easier to understand for future generations.

You don't get to ninety-five without meeting a lot of interesting people and having some interesting things happen along the way. Perhaps the secrets of my longevity shall be revealed as I write, and the story unfolds. Essentially, the longevity is down to good genes. My mother lived past one hundred and one of my grandfathers was over ninety, which was unusual for the times and the circumstances which they lived through.

Acknowledgements

I dedicate this memoir to my dear Maisie, who shared and supported my early life, my wife Chrysoulla, who has been my constant companion in later years, and my boys, Clive, Paul, Martin and their families. With thanks to my fraternity in Freemasonry, City Livery and Rotary, family and dear friends. Thank you all.

1

GETTING MY CARDS

A difficult time

The 16th July 1948 dawned dry and sunny over North London, perhaps a little cool for the time of year. It was an auspicious day, the day prior to my wedding to Maisie at St. Paul's Church, Camden Square, close to where we both lived. I was a little apprehensive but assured that I was marrying the right girl in a place that had become as familiar to me as home, amongst our family and friends. I knew Maisie would look as stunning as any princess. She worked for a company run by the designer Norman Hartnell, who were dressmakers to the future Queen, and Maisie had helped make the royal wedding dress the year before. She made her own wedding dress with help from her Hartnell's colleagues. Even if we were to be married with less pomp and circumstance than Princess Elizabeth, it was still going to be one of the most important days of my life.

It was a Friday and my last day of work before our Saturday wedding. A working day like any other. I had been at British Thomson-Houston Co (BTH) for five years, as an apprentice toolmaker and designer, attending Willesden Technical College on Saturday mornings to study for the Higher National Certificate in Engineering. I cycled to work every day from the home I shared with my parents, siblings, and tenants on Bartholomew Road, dodging through the buses and back streets of North London to my place of work on Neasden Lane, Willesden. British Thomson-Houston had a major role in developing the world's first prototype jet engine, but at that time the factory was making switchgears and parts for power stations. Later, their apprenticeships became highly thought of, but at the time it had been the only job I was offered when I left school. I could not turn it down, there was nothing else. Perhaps I didn't appreciate their kudos, but the work was not what I had dreamed of doing, I had wanted to be a musician during the war and briefly, an architect.

My development at British Thomson-Houston was stunted by the power the unions wielded. Their political opinions were extreme and opposite to my own. I would arrive at my work bench every day to find a copy of The Daily Worker newspaper lying there, even though my colleagues knew full well my sympathies did not lie with the Communist Party. I would tear it to shreds and dump it in the bin. I was less than impressed with the way the unions worked. They had prevented me from getting an individual pay rise, and I was often at loggerheads with a union that was frequently on a strike I disagreed with.

That particular Friday I was called into the foreman's office. He walked over to me and unceremoniously handed me my National Insurance and employment documents, my cards. He may have said I was being made redundant to make way for men coming back from the war, and it was to be expected. It's hard to recall, I was in shock. As I stood there holding my dismissal documents all I could think, was I wish I'd been given a bit more notice, I was getting married the next day! It was a huge blow. The marriage to Maisie and our honeymoon took my mind off it a little, but it made my future so uncertain I was determined that nothing like that would happen to me again.

My dismissal and time at that company made me more determined to work for myself and to have the flexibility to pursue my own interests. Although there was an uncertain shadow over the wedding ceremony, we went ahead, we had a happy honeymoon in Cornwall and came back to London, moving into our own small flat in Kilburn. I was lucky to find another job two days after we returned in a little place at the back of the station in Edgware, but I found my work was still marred by the unions. Voting against their strikes put me in bad books with the shop steward and I really felt like I should do something on my own. I resolved to make my own way in life and not rely on anybody else.

2

THE TIME OF CHILDHOOD

"Childhood is measured out by sounds and smells and sights,
before the dark hour of reason grows."

— *John Betjeman*

I was born on December 6th, 1925. The local midwife arrived at my birth and assisted with my delivery in my mother's upstairs bedroom at 15 Sandall Road, Kentish Town. Our family lived in that house until they were bombed out during the war. The December of my birth was part of a bitter winter. My mother told me they couldn't open the back door to the garden as the snow had drifted right up against it. The roads were blocked, and the buses and trams struggled to make headway through North London.

My parents were both born in 1893. My mother, Ivy Eveline Harmon was the matriarch of our family, in charge of the finances, and she kept a tight rein on them. My father, Sidney Walter Tuck, was one of 12 children from Islington.

Sidney's father was born in Eden Grove, next to Holloway Road Station. Opposite the station he had a butcher's shop as well as having a position as a slaughterer for Smithfield Meat Market.

My mother's father, Edward Harmon, was a herdsman at the Caledonian Road Market where the animals were slaughtered before being sent to Smithfield. This seems to be the place my parents met. Edward lived in one room of the basement of a house for the last twenty years of his life. Like a hermit living underground, he never went out. I remember taking him a tray of food once a week on Sundays with my father, descending the stone steps to his basement where he would be sat, listening to the radio. Grandfather Harmon could not read or write but he liked listening to his radio set.

My father worked as a machine minder at a printing, ink and pen works founded by the philanthropist Henry Stephens called Stephens Ink, which was next to Highbury, Arsenal's old football ground on Gillespe Road. I became supporter of Arsenal and went every week before the war with my uncle, who was not really an uncle, but the husband of a good friend of my mother's, as he had a season ticket to share. When I was a schoolboy, we were taken to matches on occasion, which made for a particularly exciting PE lesson.

My father, Sidney, went to work at Stephens Ink in a suit and tie every day, with his shoes polished and his lunch in a small briefcase. One morning he was walking to the bus stop and he ran into a neighbour who asked who it was my father worked for?

'The wife and kids.' My father quipped.

In 1925, the energy of the new century was warping into some threatening portents. Hitler published *Mein Kampf* and Mussolini dissolved the Italian parliament and named himself dictator. In England there were sparks of hope as we danced to the music of Noel Coward and Gershwin, and Virginia Woolf published Mrs Dalloway. I was born on the cusp of the first Art Deco exhibition in Paris, some of that creative atmosphere might have infused my life and influenced my eventual career choice.

Kentish Town was not as bohemian as Woolf's Bloomsbury, but it had its moments, and I had a happy childhood in Sandall Road. There was always a piano in the house. My father and my older sisters were self-taught, playing the songs of the day like 'Begin the Beguine' and my parents were fond of playing renditions of ballads from the First World War. Music was always a big part of our lives and a formative part of mine. I loved all classical music, to listen to and to play, all the well-known Violin Concertos and Gypsy Music, and later I played a lot of dance band music and became a great Opera goer.

The house on Sandall Road had a very large attic room, partitioned into three sections, one for my three older sisters and another for my mother's younger sister who lived with us until she married in 1938. The other room was mine. When my mother was 18, she lost three younger sisters and her mother all within eighteen months. Mother worked in service from the age of 14, but she had to give that up to look after the rest of the family; four younger sisters and a younger brother, who eventually lived with his father. He died in 1932 at the age of 27. She had a strong sense of family and wanted to keep us all close.

My eldest sister Renee (Irene) became a milliner, my middle sister Vera Adelaide became a shorthand typist in an office and my youngest, Muriel, became a dressmaker like my mother. There was always a black Singer sewing machine curled like a cat in the corner. It was pedal power at first, until it was fitted with an electric motor. My younger brother Peter was an electrician. We were a creative but practical family.

We lived in the end house which meant there was a long wall leading to the next road, and a long wall opposite, that made a useful base to play cricket. Any game necessitated that two boys were appointed lookouts and stationed to warn of approaching police who might box our ears. When I wasn't playing cricket against the side wall, I'd go up to the football pitches behind Regents Park on a Saturday morning, to play with friends, as long as someone had remembered to book the pitches in advance.

At the other end of the road there was a paper shop selling lemonade and bright orange Tizer in glass bottles.

The son of the shop owner was a lad about my age who joined in our cricket matches. One dark afternoon in winter he suggested we all go into his back garden and throw empty bottles from his father's shop over the wall. This meant I could get them the next day and take them back to the shop to claim the penny deposit on each one. I got a telling off for that activity and being instrumental in my friend's early criminal career. I found later that he was sent to a remand home and I never saw him again.

Our house was unheated, central heating was unknown, there was one coal fire in the sitting room, which was lit on high days and holidays, but most of the time we got our warmth from the big range in the kitchen, the room that was really the heart of the home. We had no electric lights until just before the Second World War and I would traipse up to bed on the narrow stair by candlelight, clutching a hot water bottle.

We children were not allowed to read the newspapers, but my father got the News of the World on Sundays and on Mondays I was given the job of taking the scissors to its printed pages, cutting it up into sections to be used as toilet paper in the loo. There was no bathroom in the house, baths took place in the kitchen and Friday night was our bath night when a big tin bath was placed in front of the cooking range and filled with heated water. The youngest went in first and for six years, until my brother Peter came along, that was me. Perhaps my parents thought I could go in first as I was the cleanest. After our bath, our mother gave us Ovaltine and broken biscuits that she had bought during her weekly shop at the Metropolitan Cattle Market near Caledonian Road. This was open Tuesdays and Fridays.

In the 1920s and 30s, Kentish Town and Holloway were bustling areas with a high population density, the busy main roads were crowded with shops, people and tilting high trams that ran the rail up to Parliament Hill Fields. The poet, John Betjeman, a North London lad himself, wrote of those trams, "I can remember the horse tram, open on top, and I longed to clutch one of those bobbles that hung down temptingly from the plane trees." He mentions Kentish Town in one of his more famous poems, *Parliament Hill Fields*.

When the Bon Marche was shuttered, when the feet were hot and tired,
Outside Charrington's we waited, by the 'STOP HERE IF REQUIRED'
Launched aboard the shopping basket, sat precipitately down,
Rocked past Zwanaiger the baker's, and the terrace blackish brown,
And the curious Anglo -Norman parish church of Kentish Town.

Most of the time I didn't take the tram, I walked everywhere. One day, I walked up to Parliament Hill with a group of friends. We were sixteen and full of the energies of youth. One friend had an air gun, and we took turns in taking pot shots at all sort of things, until we became aware that a Black Maria was parked behind us. The police carted us down to the local station and made us wait. Those two hours in the police station felt like a whole day to me. Eventually, they took our particulars.

"What's going to happen to us?" I queried.

"Don't know yet, we haven't decided lad." Was the answer I was given. "But we'll be round to see your parents tonight."

We all skulked home and I sat at the dinner table, queasy with apprehension and in a cold sweat. I could not eat a thing. "What's the matter with you Sidney, are you ill?" my mother asked. I dared not tell her the truth. I waited on tenterhooks all night for the knock on the door. It never came. The fear of a reprisal was warning enough, and we never took pot shots with an air gun again.

Ivy and Sidney Tuck were not keen churchgoers, but they made sure their children were. They went to church on special occasions, but otherwise they were too busy on a Sunday looking after my mother's father and Uncle George, who moved in with him after mother's brother had died. I was the one always at St. Paul's. Sometimes I was there as much as five times a day. St Paul's Church on Camden Square had a large boys' choir and a large girls' choir, and I was a key part of the former. The church was a short walk from our house, and it became a second home to me. When I was older the youth club ran dances there and I performed on the stage on my violin alongside a pianist, saxophonist, and trumpet. The church held regular whist drives which my parents attended, alongside many other activities which we were involved in as a family. St. Paul's building was severely damaged in the Second World War so it had a new building constructed, which was functional, perhaps without as much charm, but still filled with the community spirit of the congregation of the church.

The lure of the cinema was never far away when I was growing up. My sisters would take me to The Tuppenny Rush Saturday Children's Show at the art deco Kentish Town Forum and other places. We children rushed, shoved, and pushed to get to the flip down wooden seats at the front which were considered the best seats in the house for us. Hence the term, tuppenny 'rush.' We would settle, devouring our nuts from a paper twist or a sherbet dab and watch the news reels and westerns up on the big screen through the fog of cigarette smoke that hung over the audience.

The air quality outside was not much better. It was the days of thick smog in London from the factories and coal fires at home. Those days persisted for decades. In later years, I drove down to Lyons Corner House on Tottenham Court Road and could not see where I was going. The air didn't really improve until the clean air act in the early Sixties which limited coal fires. I remember the coal man calling to deliver a ton of coal at our house, we kids would stand by and count the sacks as he sent them down the coal chute from the pavement to the basement, where mum did all the household washing on Mondays and the washing for her uncle and my grandfather. I don't know how she managed to get it all dry outside, and not covered in coal smuts. There was a pulley maid in the kitchen over the range which was often full of damp washing flapping like wet pastry.

Sidney Tuck (Father) in Uniform (1914)>

Ivy Tuck (Mother) (1914)

Sidney with Teddy age 3 (1928)

Sidney Outside Sandall Road, London, starting school age 5 (1930)

The Tuck Family at the End of The War (1945)

3

TIME FOR SCHOOL

When the time came to go to school I attended Hungerford Road Primary, less than a ten minute walk up the hill of Camden Road, just past the Lord Stanley pub, which I frequented in later life with many a pint after church. Hungerford Road was an imposing, several story Victorian building that looked like a castle. In class, we sat in rows at wooden desks each with its own inkwell. The girl in front of me had long plaits and one day, as her blond hair swung, the temptation was too much, I snatched the ends of her hair and dipped them into the black ink in my well. I was sent to stand in the corner of the playground until home time.

I walked through the back streets to my second school, Lyulph Stanley Central in Crowndale Road. Central schools were set-up by the London County Council back in 1911 to teach commercial or technical subjects to the industrial classes. Pupils started the school aged 11 and normally stayed for four years. I was taught woodwork and metalwork and German, as well as maths and there was also a music class. I had been offered music lessons at primary school and I chose to learn to play the violin, which made a significant impact on the development of my musical ability. I continued with my violin at Lyulph Stanley and passed the examination for playing in 'The Higher Grade' with the Maidstone Violin Classes of Great Britain. I still have most of my school reports, and the neat, tiny writing makes me out to be better in some subjects than I was, apart from maths, which I did do well in. I had many friends there including the actor, Kenneth Williams, whose father had a Barbers Shop in Pratt Street. Even then Kenneth was the comic and made us all laugh.

Like most people's school days, I had happy times and not so happy times. There were bullies, as there are in many walks of life, and a few made my life a misery at Lyulph Stanley. At the end of one term, one of them started on me in the playground and it developed into a full-blown fist fight. Thankfully, some of my friends from my scout group came to my aid. I don't know how it happened, but when I threw a punch at the bully, he collapsed. By the time a teacher arrived and brought him around, I'd had my name taken and was told I would be dealt with after the holidays. When we went back to school after the holidays nothing happened, except the bullying stopped.

Around 1937, I won a scholarship and moved to the North Western Polytechnic on Prince of Wales Road. It was a big school with more than 2,200 students, engaged mainly in evening classes, and an academic staff of 150, concentrating on social sciences, humanities, and the arts. It evolved to the present-day London Metropolitan University on Holloway Road.

When the war started in September 1939, I was evacuated to Luton with most of my school and we attended The Luton Modern school, a new school then, situated at the foot of a hill leading up to the old aerodrome at Stopsley. That hill was a favourite place for boys in winter to rocket down on sledges on snowy days. My studies at The Luton School were engineering based; maths, algebra and trigonometry, but I continued with music in lunchtime lessons. I discovered later after I met my wife Maisie, that she had been billeted just around the corner from me, yet we never met.

My evacuation was a well organised affair, and could have been so much worse, but I was lucky. My family took me to Kentish Town station, and I knew I would see them again soon, I was home most weekends to sing in the church choir. The vicar paid my train fares so I could get back for weddings and practices. I was just shy of 14 years old, so not a young child and I had a level of maturity and a little experience of the world that others may not have had. When all the evacuees arrived in Luton, we were paraded in a line on the platform and the locals picked out who they wanted. My younger brother Peter went elsewhere to a farm in Gamlingay. I was left standing alone until I was chosen.

My second billet was with a local schoolmaster, Mr. Griggs, who was also a director of Luton Football Club. He lived about five minutes' walk from my Luton school in a modest three bed semi-detached house. He and his wife had no children and I found it quite different being an only child from being part of a house full of my family in London. In later life, I discovered that Mr. Griggs was a Grand Officer of The Masons, so perhaps it was serendipitous that I lived with them for a time, yet whether it had any subconscious influence on my future involvement with The Masons I do not know.

Usually evacuees were billeted two together and there was another lad from school I was friendly with whose mother lived opposite Parliament Hill Fields. Peter's family had just moved to a new housing estate at Sundon while his father was away with the navy, so I moved in with them and Peter. We walked to school together, several miles a day through the open countryside, crossing streams and trying not to fall in. Peter's grandparents lived with them and his grandmother told fortunes. She read my palm, and everything she predicted came true; married twice, a serious illness, and that I would live to a very great age.

We had many good lessons at Luton Modern School, and we were sent up to the technical college for metalwork. We enjoyed the new facilities at Luton, including the open playing fields, our teachers from London had been evacuated with us and one was an ex-Arsenal footballer and took us for football on those fields. Luton was a rural area at that time, and we enjoyed the open fields and lanes that were so different to our London streets, and the clean, country air instead of the London smog. The local school pupils accepted us evacuees, and I made friends easily. In fact, I made good friends there. We'd traipse to the local tuckshop to buy sweets together and watch the training of air pilots at the top of the hill. The airport was a base for 264 Fighter Squadron during the war, as well as a manufacturing site where both civil and military aircraft were designed and built.

Back at home, London was enduring the Blitz. My family at Sandall Road were bombed out in one of the earliest raids in 1941. During raids they headed to the safest place in the house which was under the table in the kitchen. They were under there when a bomb went down the chimney of the house next door and came down around their ears, leaving the brick walls flapping with loose wallpaper. They were lucky to escape alive. My parents went up to the church half a mile away which served as a shelter for homeless refugees, until they found somewhere else to live. The lady they had rented the house from on Sandall Road gave them another house around the corner, on Bartholomew Road. A three-storey white and brick Victorian town house with sash windows, high steps to the front door and a basement. My mother sublet the top floor of that house and I remember the people who rented it, an elderly couple named Upstone who kept themselves to themselves, so we did not see much of them. In the sixties, my parents moved from Bartholomew Road to a small, one bedroomed ground floor flat in Rochester Road. I moved back to Bartholomew Road after evacuation at the end of the war and did not leave home again until I got married.

At Lyulph Stanley, I had progressed with the violin and when I qualified, I was enlisted into the London Schools Orchestra and played at Queen's Hall when Sir Henry Wood was the conductor. I later performed at Wembley Town Hall as a member of Wembley Philharmonic Orchestra. I remember rehearsing with the orchestra for a Christmas concert and the singer arrived to begin his piece. The conductor, who was an important conductor who worked for the BBC, stopped the orchestra dead.

"We can't hear you." He said

"Well I haven't got a microphone." The singer replied. The conductor looked around at the vaulted ceiling of the hall and sighed.

"You don't need one in a place like this, you should be able to cope or you can go home." The singer went home. The Conductor found another singer at very short notice. Some other concerts I performed in moved to the Royal Albert Hall which became the permanent home of the Henry Wood Promenade Concerts in 1946.

When I came back to London towards the end of the war,

I started to attend an evening class in music at The Burley Road School. The principal teacher there was Dan Franks, a fairly elderly musician who taught and played the violin and several wind instruments. He suggested that it might be a good idea for me to learn a wind instrument too, so he loaned me his French horn, which I then bought out of the money he was paying me to perform. That French horn was passed to my eldest son, Clive, who passed it on to his son Simon. I then purchased a French Horn for my youngest son, Martin. It is now with my granddaughter in Kansas, who plays it regularly.

Dan Franks had a brass band and an orchestra, and I played in both. We alternated with afternoon concerts on Sundays in Regents Park Zoo, where we would crowd into the bandstand as the great, grey barrage balloons floated overhead. When we heard the drone of doodlebugs, we'd halt whatever we were performing and hit the deck, scrabbling to get down on the wooden floor below our music stands. When the doodlebugs passed, we climbed back up, straightened our music, and carried on playing. We also played for the Passion Plays that were part of the Easter parade at Holy Joe's (St. Joseph's Catholic Church, Highgate) and one in East London. St. Joseph's invited us back to the church after the parade, where they had barrels of beer lined up in the crypt. Playing the French horn was thirsty work and Holy Joe's proved good at quenching that thirst. Church was where I learned to drink beer!

There was a shortage of musicians during the war as most had joined the forces, so at least once a week I was asked to fill in playing the fiddle with a few others in a gypsy band at Lyons Corner House, or occasionally at The Clarendon Hotel, Hammersmith. We'd squash between packed tables while waitresses buzzed around us in their white caps and collars and perform at the tables for customers celebrating special occasions like birthday parties, there was always a drink waiting for us on our return to our corner, as a reward.

My music career expanded when I went to join the British Legion in Marylebone.

"But you haven't been in the army, you can't join." They said.

"I'm a musician." I replied, as if that would be reason enough.

"Well you can play in the band then." And so began years of playing as an unofficial British Legion member in the band at military occasions like the annual remembrance services at the cenotaph at the end of the war when we led the Boer War veterans. My commitment to musical performances did peter out after I got married and other organisational responsibilities took over, but I continued to play for the Wembley Philharmonic Orchestra until we moved to St. Albans.

Me Playing the Violin, age 16

4

TIME TO MEET A SOULMATE

When I dream of you
My dreams are always sheer delights
Of things that are and will be
Perfect happiness in sight.

I am sorry when I waken
And the day begins anew
But I revel in your company
When I dream of you

— *Maisie Tuck, 1949*

I met my wife, Maisie, through music. I was attending evening classes at Burley Road School and she was taking operatic classes. The orchestra I belonged to supported the singers. Maisie wrote to me not long after we met to suggest a party at her friends.

"Do you think we could go after 'The Gondoliers'? We will probably have to stay the night, only I thought you ought to know so that you can tell your ma. Do you think you will be too tired? I hope not because you can give us all a tune over there." Maisie remarked that she only knew one or two notes of the opera of 'The Gondoliers', but that it was ten times better than 'The Pirates', meaning the Pirates of Penzance. Maisie was fond of Gilbert and Sullivan generally, and we used to go to a hotel in Stanmore where they would have singers perform songs from the operas during dinner. The hotel was originally Mr Gilbert's home.

Maisie Isabel Boyce was born October 1st, 1926, to parents Emily Boyce (nee Daniel) and Arthur Boyce. They lived at Hawley Crescent, NW1, and moved just before the war to 78 Kenbrook House, in a block of council flats on Leighton Road, NW5. She had an older brother George, a stepbrother Bill and a stepsister Phyllis. Maisie's father, Arthur Boyce, was in the Cavalry Regiment which had barracks near Regents Park. When he retired, he worked for The Post Office, and by the time I met Maisie he was a nightwatchman at the main Post Office on Mount Pleasant. I do not remember him as being an unkind parent, but all his offspring remember when he arrived home at night, they would all run immediately to bed.

Maisie lived just two hundred yards down the road from our house, so she was almost the quintessential girl next door. I started walking her home after her evening class, spending longer and longer lingering on the stairs at Kenbrook House together, until one day she sprung it upon me.

"My father's seen you walking me home Sidney. He wants to meet you." I suppose he wanted to know who his daughter was stepping out with and what my intentions were. We met, and he seemed to like me, so Maisie and I continued to see each other and started going to the cinema and courting properly. Maisie kept a diary, and she detailed our blossoming relationship. Although we had met on coming home from evening classes, I must have mentioned the Victory Dance which was to be held at the Church Hall in Camden Square on Saturday, June 10th, 1945, and for this, I get a first mention in her diary.

"Had good time and came home with Sidney," Maisie's daily diaries draw a picture of our developing relationship against the background of the post-war years. We met once or twice a week after I first walked her home.

On Sunday, July 8th, she came with me to Poplar where I was playing in the Dan Franks Orchestra and our Friday nights at the Church Club of St. Pauls became a regular fixture. We played badminton, table tennis and card games there. The Club was run by a Governess type lady called Mrs Le Mesurier who had lost her husband in the First World War and had connections with the Star and Garter, a home that was looking after wounded servicemen. Once a year Maisie and I were involved with entertaining the coachload of veterans with tea and cakes, followed by a singalong of well-known songs. Maisie's diaries show glimpses of how Britain was changing post-war. She mentions the street lighting resuming on July 17th after having been off for the whole of the War. Sunday August 5th, was the first day Maisie met my family. She records it as. "Went to Southend with Mum to Sidney, Mr & Mrs Tuck and Peter. Had a good day together."

Our meetings became more and more frequent, we went to dances, on walks to Kenwood and to the proms at The Royal Albert Hall. I was obviously quite shy, and it took me a little time to make my move, as Maisie says on October 5th, 1945. "Went to work. Went to Club. Came home with Sidney. Sidney gave me a x."

By 1946 we were meeting for films or walks nearly every day. We went to see a new Lauren Bacall film in early 1946, after which Maisie confided in her diary that she was never wrapped up in a film when she was sitting next to me, her mind was on me all the time, not the film. She was devoted to me, and I to her.

In the Spring of 1946 Maisie was coming home from work on her bike when she was hit by a car. She was taken to St. Georges Hospital where they operated on her leg. After a very disturbing night, the gentleman who knocked her down came to see her and she records me visiting almost every day. She was moved to Atkinson Morley Hospital in Wimbledon for Convalescence and enjoyed many visitors there. By June she was recovering quickly and she returned home on the 14th and I took her to the church club that evening.

A week later, she went to see my mother and took her to The Tivoli, my parents were always fond of Maisie and she always said my pa made her laugh. The next day we went to the church club and afterwards several our members came with us and celebrated Maisie's return by going for a drink at The Lord Stanley pub, which had become my regular post church.

Maisie often came to hear me play the French Horn in the Brass Band, sometimes at Paddington Recreational Grounds, Wandsworth Common or Blackwall Palace Gardens. She loved to watch me play French horn or violin, even before we officially met. Once we were a couple, Maisie mentioned how much she liked to hear me pay the fiddle. Once we stayed in rather than go to the pictures, as her brother George had turned up with his guitar, and we made an impromptu band, me on the fiddle, George on guitar and Maisie on comb and paper!

The Fiddle

You be the fiddle and I'll be the bow
We must be together wherever we go
Without one another, we never could play
The wonderful music we hear of today

If the fiddle and bow are kept apart
The fiddle will cease, for the bow is its heart
A heartless fiddle has lost its tone
Because of no bow, it is all alone

A bow on its own can produce no sound
In silence, it waits, till its fiddle is found
Where is the fiddler who makes us as one?
While we're apart his work is not done

Who is this fiddler with power so strong?
We're kept apart by him for so long
Love is our fiddler, so if we are true
He'll keep us together and be with us too

— Maisie

I have seldom played the violin since Maisie died.

By the end of that ten-week period, Maisie and I were seeing each other every day. July 9th was rather a special day for Maisie and her involvement with the Girl Guides, she went to St. Pancras Town Hall to form a guard of honour for the Queen and Princess Margaret, and The Queen spoke to Maisie. She then was away for a short time visiting her aunt and uncle in Leeds, but I went to meet her off the train when she got back.

After she met my family and I met hers, as in so many areas, most people knew each other, and when Maisie cycled her bike to work through St. John's Wood, she pulled up by the milkman one day.

"I know you, don't I?" she said.

"I know you." He replied, "You're Sidney's girl, I'm married to his middle sister" They exchanged pleasantries as they passed each day.

I had lots of friends at school who were in the forces and whenever they came home we'd have a night out in Leicester Square and walk home, sometimes during a raid, although it was mainly doodle bugs towards the end of the war and less devastating. We'd sleep down Kentish Town tube station when I came home for the weekend from my evacuation billet. The vicar of St. Pauls would pay my train fare back, I was often back at weekends to sing with the choir at the weddings in St. Pauls' church, and paid for doing so. Eventually I got a paper round and used the pay to save up and buy a bicycle, which meant I could ride home after school Friday and return Sunday evening.

Returning to London for work, I started going back to my old haunts. The church choir, the youth club at St. Pauls and seeing my school friends. We'd all started work at the same time. One of my workmates was quite heavily involved in scouting at a church in Paddington and suggested I might like to help running the troop. I agreed and was soon going one night a week and taking the boys on camps in the summer. The scouts also volunteered to help the nurses at the hospital, and a rota was set up for evenings and weekends.

The next big occasion of those years was December 6th, 1946, which was my 21st Birthday and the day I got engaged to Maisie. We had talked about getting married for over two years, and I know she was impatient for us to be together, and not to have to leave me each night on the stairs by her flat. We went out and bought an engagement ring and went to an old school friend's wedding later that month as fiancés. That was Arthur Bowen who lived next door to me in Bartholomew Road and had gone into shipping with P&O. He eventually progressed to Director in charge of freight, and as the company did a lot of business with Jordan, he became Secretary of The Jordanian Society and joined Freemasonry just after me.

Maisie and I kept a joint diary for our wedding and honeymoon. It had been a long courtship, not without its obstacles, hinted at in Maisie's diaries, she sometimes mentioned how my mother would exercise her dominance over me and it frustrated her.

"I think it's about time your mother realised that you are to be shared with others." She said. But we got there in the end. We were married in our beloved St. Paul's, I waited at the altar at 2pm. Maisie should have been in church, but she was late. I dared not turn around to see if she was coming, and then I heard the organ strike up 'Here Comes the Bride' at ten past, and I could feel Maisie coming towards me. Father Wells gave us a lovely service and there were hundreds of photographs after.

We stayed the night at our newly procured flat, which was above that of Mab and George, before we headed down to Cornwall on the train from Paddington traveling first-class to ensure we got seats. When we opened our cases, someone had packed an empty gin bottle and a crust of bread. Someone had stuck 'Just Married' on one side of the case and as the train pulled from the station we were smothered in confetti. We were still finding it the next morning when our Cornish landlady brought us a cup of tea in bed. We walked to Porthleven and sat on the seat above the cliff top while the sea battered the cliffs below and the spray bloomed into our faces.

It was a lovely honeymoon. We played tennis, improving over time, walked on Praa Sands, found small pubs for Cornish ale and persuaded an old seaman to take us out in his boat, he gave us a tour of the coastline and we gave him a bob. The memories of that time I have kept forever.

This world will go on forever and ever
Time never changes a love that is true
Dearest of all the husbands that are
I'll be happy forever if you're happy too

— *Maisie*

Maisie

Myself and Maisie

With the Bridesmaids – Maisie's Work Colleague, Stepsister and My Niece, Valerie

My Father, Sidney, On the Far Left, Muriel, Ivy, Maisie With Her Brother George Behind, Her Father, Arthur Boyce and Her Mother

The Mikado, Three Little Maids. Maisie On the Far Right

A Collection of Miniature Photos from Our Holidays

5

TIME MOVES ON

The mechanism of work and career

It doesn't just tell time, it tells history

— Rolex advertising

was interested in clocks and watches from childhood and often to be found taking an object apart and examining the mechanics because I was fascinated by how things worked. I'd have a go at dismantling crystal radio sets to examine their inner workings and was attracted to all mechanisms and their delicate operations. I knew from an early age it was something I wanted to work with. At Lyulph Stanley School I was entered for a competition for blacksmithing and as the years passed, I realised that toolmaking would suit me. I was in the right environment for it, Lyle Stanley was a trade school, and we were trained in the basics of engineering, and the Polytechnic expanded its higher grades in Maths etc. When it came time to leave, I was offered the apprenticeship with BTH, although it was the only thing I was offered, there was no alternative. I had entertained the idea of being an architect, nothing in that line was available to me, and I put those thoughts aside as I began my apprenticeship, although I did build a sun lounge on the back of our house and removed a wall between two rooms at Evelyn Avenue.

Before engineering or horology, I had other dreams too, of being a musician, but those would have to wait, there were other things looming on the horizon. We were deep into the Second World War when at eighteen, myself and ten of my friends eagerly trotted up to the RAF recruitment centre to sign up. We took the tests and were all accepted, I still have my medical pass certificate. I expected to get a letter telling me where I had to report to sign up, but the letter never came. I wasn't allowed to leave along with my friends, as the engineering apprenticeship I was doing at BTH making aircraft parts and power station equipment was deemed essential to war work.

My interest in all things mechanical persisted throughout my early career, until eventually I became something of a self-taught horologist. When I had any spare time, I would fix watches for the family, for my wife and her brothers, until I became the go-to repair person and fixed up a little workbench in the corner of one room in our house. Until one day, a friend said to me.

"You can't keep doing all these repairs at home, the payments are going to show up in your bank account and it might look suspicious, you'd better tell the tax people." So, I registered with the Inland Revenue and made it official.

After I got my cards from British Thompson Houston, and returned from honeymoon, I eventually found another position with Mica and Micanite Ltd. where I made tools to make parts for valves and wires and worked on the development of the machine to build those tiny valves. In 1954, I bought a car from my friend Paul Ungar. Paul and I had met at St. Paul's Church through the Scout group. Paul was from Vienna in Austria where his mother had a high-class ladies dress shop. They saw which way the wind was blowing across Europe in the late thirties with the rise of fascism, and they left everything behind in 1938 to come to England. Paul trained at the famous Moorfields Eye Hospital and eventually became our family optician. The car I bought from him was a small, standard ten, made by the British Standard Motor company. I acquired my licence which meant I could drive from work in the Mica Micanite factory in Barnsbury Square to Clerkenwell in my lunch hour to get spare parts for the watches I was repairing. I'd pop into a nearby pub for a pie and a pint and drive back to work.

Maisie had set up our own home and were living quite happily at Brondesbury Road, Kilburn. But when our first son, Clive Daniel Sidney was born, we were trapped in the flat. We had no garden, and we wanted to buy a house. Maisie wrote about what sort of home she would like us to have:

My home must always have a cobweb that has missed the dusters touch
My bookshelves must not be too neat as if nobody has used them much
There must be signs of wear in places proving friends have called and stayed
A stray toy or some open music
Reminding me of pleasures made

We had a few hundred saved and went to an estate agent in Southgate to see what he could do for us. We didn't like anything he showed us, they were all terrible places, and he must have got fed up with our requests, because he snapped.

"You're wasting my time, don't bother coming back to me unless you've got at least another hundred." He had Maisie in tears he was that unpleasant. At the time, The Masons were talking about buying a hall in Southgate, and who would turn out to be the chairman at the hall but the same estate agent! Just shows you should be kind to everyone you meet on your journey through life, as you never know when they might be able to help you.

Finally, in 1952 we found a house. A post war, bay fronted Terraced House on Evelyn Avenue in Kingsbury. We bought it for £2,150, with a mortgage from The Portman Building Society for £2,000. We stayed in that house quite a while and I got planning permission to build a garage, a loft conversion, and a sun lounge with a wine cellar underneath. Our first son, Clive Daniel Sidney was born at Kingsbury Maternity Hospital, and our second son followed at home in 1953, Paul Edward Ernest, he now lives in Brookmans Park.

There was blip in my early career at Mica Micanite when in September 1957, I was rushed to Edgware hospital to have my appendix out. There was no telephone communication, so Maisie wrote me a letter while I was there, although she had visited me on the ward. She told me when I was at home, how she missed my companionship and when I was away everything seemed empty.

"There isn't much one can say in a ward full of people is there? I know now how you must have felt when I was away from you for ten days when I had Clive". I had written to her at Kingsbury Maternity Hospital when she had our first son. It was the first time we had been away from each other since we were married, when I wrote in our honeymoon diary, "The day when we start a long, and ideally happy married life together." My letter tells Maisie that it was.

"A happy thought that Clive came into the world through our love and through our continued love will continue to grow to be both respected and respectful to others." Babies were taken away from their mothers and put in the nursery after birth, which I had not been present at, so I had not seen Maisie holding Clive, and longed for them both to come home. I signed my name at the end of my letter and spelled out 'I love you darling.' in kisses.

My career progressed within engineering at Mica Micanite, but I felt I was not doing what I wanted. I was restless working for somebody else and I experienced ongoing struggles with the unions. What else could I do? I thought. Well, I could repair watches, so when I saw an ad in the paper for a bankrupt Jewellery business in Finchley, I was very tempted. I had some hard thinking and negotiating to do. The jewellers at 6 Station Road was for sale for £125. I had some £100 in the building society and approached Lloyds Bank for a loan for the remaining £25.

However, I was to find a better deal. I had some Jewish friends through the lodge, one of whom was an accountant.

"I'll introduce you to my bank." He said and took me to Barclays at Willesden Green. The manager there was helpful. "We'll take over your mortgage." He offered "And we won't put the fees up any more than two and a half percent." They did this, and they lent me £125 to purchase the business. I was beginning to find how useful my contacts could be. The introduction enabled me to buy the shop, leave Mica Micanite, and begin my career as a jeweller.

Just before I had seen the ad for the Finchley shop, I had seen an advert for a new town with shops available to rent and put in an offer for one. Stevenage was the first of the new towns to be built after the war, it was planned with six self-contained neighbourhoods of housing, shops, and green spaces. In 1956, within twelve months of buying Finchley, the offer of the shop in Stevenage came through. Like the expanding acquisition of property in a Monopoly game, my modest empire was growing, but the Stevenage shop was going to cost me more than Finchley. It would be £500. I went to the bank again and they agreed to let me have the money. I still have all the documents typed in triplicate, on yellowing paper bound with a red ribbon. I finally opened the Stevenage shop in 1958. It was built from scratch as part of the new town and I still have the plans for it.

By the late 1950s I had finally found a working life that suited me. I would drive to my shop at 8.30am and get the jewellery out of the overnight safe and set the window up like a glittering chocolate box of delights. I employed a manager for the Stevenage shop, a chap who used to work for Hinds jewellers, and started him on £8.10 a week, which was a good salary at the time. I worked one day in Finchley, one in Stevenage and would come home from either to read to the boys before they went to bed. Family life was important and that was our special time, sharing stories that were mostly adventure tales from the popular authors of the time like Enid Blyton, before I'd come down for dinner with Maisie and then sit up till 2am doing watch repairs before going to work the next day. I would do all the stocktaking and buying for the shop, but it got so busy in Stevenage that we couldn't handle all the repairs and employed five more watchmakers to help.

The exclusive stock was expensive to purchase, but we must have been good customers as the bank manager used to take me out for dinner every year at a local pub. Although I was limited in what stock I could buy at the beginning, I never had much spare money to buy it. I had to go to the bank manager.

"You're keeping your head above water Sidney, but why didn't you tell me you were a Freemason?" He said. I was surprised he knew.

"We're not supposed to go around telling people." I said. The Masons were a much more secretive organisation at the time.

"I found out because I see the cheques you write to pay your dues." He said. By this time, my Barclays branch had moved to an imposing building with marble floors and classical columns on Victoria Street in London. Once he saw I was a Mason, the manager saw to it that I was introduced to some of his bigger clients. Ingersoll's and others would send me stock, and as I sold it, I would pay them, and they would replace the stock.

The jewellery business changed in the 1960s when the quartz battery watch was invented and the market was suddenly flooded with cheap watches, you could get one as a gift when you bought petrol, or with your green shield stamps. Within a couple of weeks, we saw the demand for clockwork watches plummet. Watchmakers disappeared, there was no need for their services any more as the industry irreversibly changed.

We were able to maintain some exclusive contracts throughout this period, our shop in Stevenage had the only licence to sell Rolex. However, in the Finchley shop we could sell these prestigious watches, but we were not allowed to put them on display in the window. Our regular customers knew we stocked them though and would ask me to bring samples to their homes to examine, like Jack Cohen, the founder of Tesco, who lived in Finchley. Jack would come into the shop and select a few Rolex to take away with him, or he'd call and ask me to deliver some to his mansion on the Saturday morning. Cliff Richard was also a regular client.

Our excellent customer base expanded through the late 1950s as Maisie's mother cleaned for a number of families in St. John's Wood, a high-class area of North London. She would mention her son-in-law was a jeweller and refer them to me for business. I used to repair all their clocks and watches. Some client relationships were beneficial, one of our clients was friends with a piano teacher called Hilda Bor, who used to go to Buckingham Palace to teach

Prince Charles and Princess Anne. My eldest son had told me he wanted to learn to play the piano, so Hilda agreed to teach him. There were other distinguished musicians in the area who became our clients too, a harpist, whose name escapes me, whenever she answered the door to me, she was smoking a pipe. There were many Jewish families who lived in St. John's Wood who became good clients. Some were our neighbours and looked after our cat when we went on holiday. I'd leave the cat food out, a well-known brand with the tin marked with a single paw print. I told them., "No need to worry, you'll find his food, the Rabbi Cat has signed his name on it."

The 1950s and '60s were a hectic time for me and the family. We had a new house that took two years to organise the purchase, two businesses and two young sons. We were so busy with commitments, that it was rare for us to meet up with friends, except for Doris and Bill Cottle, who bought a house just a short distance away and were regular church goers alongside ourselves, and active in the village church in Kingsbury. The shops were doing well, and we began to expand our services. Perhaps inspired by Maisie's way with words, I placed a poem in the local paper as an advertisement.

Mary, Mary, quite contrary
Went to buy a watch
She'd been warned about another store

But did not care a jot
She bought an expensive looking watch, expensive price as well
But after a week or so
The time it refused to tell
She returned it to the store at once
Worried without a doubt
'It will take a week' they said, 'we have to send it out.'
She wished she'd taken good advice
And gone to buy from TUCK
Whose stock of watches are handpicked
And the need of any service is not left to luck
TRY TUCK THE JEWELLERS – THE ROLEX AGENCY

A decade later I started to offer ear piercings at Stevenage, registering my hygiene and proficiency. A notice in the window declared, 'Ears pierced while you wait.'

As the years passed, I became more and more involved with the Masons alongside work. My membership of the organisation was to change my career. In 1975, a friend who was a member of one of my lodges and worked for Barr's Drinks, who made Tizer, came to see me. Peter was sales manager and had to increase his turnover every year, that year he had not managed it and they sacked him. He was 40.

"Can I come and work for you Sidney?" he asked

"I can't afford you Peter."

"Oh, I don't want paying, you can teach me the business."

Peter did come to work for me for a couple of years and it proved to be a serendipitous move. There were frequent break ins at the Finchley shop, and it was common for me to be called out at all hours, often twice in one week. After one call out when I was making my way to the shop at 2am on empty roads, I got a speeding fine. That felt like the last straw. The thieves never took much as everything was in the safe, but I was getting tired of it and complained to Peter.

"I'm fed up with all these break ins, I've got to give it up." To my surprise, he said.

"I'll buy it. I can't pay you all you want, but I'll pay you what I can, and I'll get a loan for the rest." He arranged to pay me monthly over 3 years, in the end a total of £5,000. Not a bad increase on my initial £125 investment, although this did include some stock.

Clive at 2 Years Old (1952)

Established 1900

H. E. VINCENT

Watchmaker, Jeweller and Optician

Repairs of Every Description   Under Personal Supervision

13557

STATION ROAD
FINCHLEY, N.3

16th Sept. 1957

Received of Mr Turch £125 (Hundred and Twenty Five Pounds) for Stock at 6, Station Church End, Finchley

A E Vincent

Receipt for the Purchase of the Finchley Jewellers, 1957

6

CEREMONIAL TIME

The Freemasons and other organisations

"The strength of Freemasonry is in its loyalty to each other."
— *Vasilios Karpos*

From the time we met, Maisie and I were both incredibly involved in St. Paul's Church with the youth club and our respective scout and guide groups. I had been in the scouts there myself when I was younger. This continued with the Paddington Church after moving to Kingsbury. Our involvement with the church was important to me, and the significance of ritual and a strong faith influenced my involvement with other organisations. I had a number of friends from Lyulph Stanley School at St. Pauls, and a couple had joined The Masons. I knew nothing about Freemasonry in the early 1950s, but when I mentioned to my father that I was thinking of joining, he told me he thought it was a good thing as his employer, Henry Stephens of Stephens Ink, was a member, and it seemed to have made him a good boss.

My friends persuaded me I could afford to join the Masons when I was invited. On my 31st birthday in 1956, I was initiated into the Esoteric Lodge, number 6774. I went to speak to my foreman at Mica & Micanite about having some time off so I could attend my Initiation.

"I need next Thursday afternoon off." I asked. He shook his head.

"Oh, I can't give you that Sidney, you'll have to speak to The Governor." I went up to Mr. Bergle and repeated my request.

"Why do you want this time off?" He said.

"I might need more regular time off, some afternoons and evenings, I've got a new commitment." I said. Mr. Bergle peered at me.

"Is this likely to happen often?" I shifted from foot to foot, how to explain that it was likely to happen often, without revealing what was supposed to be a secret.

"About five times a year Mr. Bergle."

"Wouldn't be Freemasonry would it?" he said. He'd found me out, I had to confess.

"Yes it would."

"Well, you can have any time off you like then, don't tell anyone else what's it for though Sidney." He warned. So began my long career in the service of the freemasons. I had no idea when I joined that Freemasonry would have such a huge influence on my life and become a complete career of itself.

My initiation was held at Lyons Corner House on Tottenham Court Road and cost me the princely sum of eighteen guineas, with an annual fee of five guineas (just over £5 in today's money). The corner houses were huge, with restaurants on four or five levels and each employed something like 400 staff. Every floor had its own restaurant style, and all had orchestras playing to the diners almost continuously throughout the day and evening. I had played there myself as part of a Gypsy Band in the 1940's. Our lodge in the top room was established and archaic to some extent, where we held four meetings a year inclusive of a meal. A guest would cost 12/6, for a three-course meal followed by brandy and a cigar. When the Lyons Corner House closed in 1966 the lodge moved to The Commonwealth Club and we spent many happy years there. Escalating costs meant we had to look for a more affordable venue and we found a permanent new home at Southgate Masonic Centre on the High Street in Southgate, North London.

This had come about after protracted searching and organisational structuring. In April 1963, a number of Middlesex Masons (who were also London Masons) decided to set up a private Company with the express intent of providing a permanent home; the Middlesex Masonic

Centre, in the North of the province. The company was duly incorporated, with a share issue of 2000 shares at £1 each, and it was named The North Middlesex Masonic Centre. Any lodge wishing to meet at the centre could do so by purchasing 1000 shares. By May 1964, the initial shareholding of 2000 was near to being taken up and a further 48,000 shares of £1 each were issued. Many popular meeting places in and around Barnet were beginning to close their doors to Freemasonry at the time and it was agreed to widen the scope of the use of the proposed centre. The search became more vigorous. On July 14th, 1967, the chairman of the company signed the contract to purchase in the sum of £43,500, though there was still a lack of funds. The Grand Lodge refused to give financial assistance, saying that the centre must stand on its own feet. Finally, a private loan was arranged, and the purchase was complete in February 1968. A resolution was passed at an extraordinary general meeting that the name of the company be changed to Southgate Masonic Centre Limited and it was able to operate in neutral territory. I was involved with negotiations and meetings to enable the foundation of the new centre and served on the board of directors of the company.

My involvement in high office was to come, and could not have been predicted, when back in 1956, shortly after my initiation, I was asked to give one of the toasts at short notice. I was apprehensive, unaccustomed to public speaking, and more than a little daunted. I felt it wasn't for me. On the way to the meeting I picked up one of the older members in my car and told him of my reluctance to speak, so much so that I had written my resignation with the intention of handing it in after the meeting.

"Do you have it with you now? If you give it to me Sidney, I'll make sure it gets to the right place." He said. I fumbled in my pocket and brought out my resignation letter and handed it over. He promptly tore it to shreds. "This is the right place Sidney." He said. He was right, within the year my fear of public speaking had disappeared, thanks in no small part to the efforts of Maisie, who was active in amateur dramatics, and coached me on diction and projection for a performance.

There were a lot of rituals to learn in The Masons, and a member passed through several offices before finally doing well enough to be elected to the ultimate office of Master of the Lodge. In 1967 I had reached the office of Junior Warden, which allowed me to attend the quarterly meetings of the Grand Lodge held at Great Queen Street in Holborn, London, right in The City. I was not at the level where I could stay for lunch, but I parked close by and could drive back to Finchley to enjoy lunch with the Rotary Club instead, a journey of fifteen minutes in 1960s traffic.

I was finally installed as Master in May 1967, which created visits to other lodges and expanded my network of duties. Appointments were frequent and demanding, hard to juggle alongside family and career, and I would often send my apologies, as I could not attend. However, Masonry becomes one big family, members and wives would communicate frequently and it was quite common for me to get back from work to be faced with a disgruntled wife who told me that, "so and so rang today and mentioned you sent apologies for the meeting, why did you do that Sidney?"

"I thought I was going out a little too often." Maisie obviously took my obligations more seriously than I did and reprimanded me.

"I told them you would be there."

She provided great support and ensured my continued involvement with the lodge. Once a year the Lodge had a Ladies Night to honour the Masters' Lady. Maisie and all the family attended, and during the dinner we had an interval when Clive, our son, gave a Piano Recital. All present enjoyed it and a few days later, Clive had a letter from Sidney Gregg the owner of Gregg's bakery, (one of our members) enclosing a cheque for £100 to put it away to go towards a Piano when Clive got married, which he did on September 14th, 1974.

The Masonic organisation creates discipline in its members, as I discovered when I became Secretary of the Lodge. When a new master was installed, a form had to be filled in notifying the Grand Lodge of details of the officers. One time we had the installation a few days before the grand lodge was to meet, and I attended, making my way to my seat, when I was stopped and called into the office of the Grand Secretary, Sir James Stubbs. He chastised me for the fact that we were having our meeting a few days before and a certain brother had signed in as master of our lodge and the records did not agree. I explained the meeting was a few days prior and they had obviously not received the important form I had posted a few days after. Sir James shook the form at me.

"This should be sent immediately, not two or three days after." I considered myself reprimanded and remembered the procedure in future. There were many such steps in the organisation, and although Kafkaesque at times, there was a reason and a logic to them.

Some years later I had a call from Sir James Stubbs. He had retired by then and heard I was a horologist. He asked me to visit his house and have a look at his grandfather clock, which had been repaired three times by someone and was still not working. I drove down to see him in London to find the clock was indeed broken, but as it was a grandfather clock it was one of the easier mechanisms to work on. I managed to mend it and he offered me a drink and confessed that some had found him difficult in the Masonic craft, but he had to always be firm in carrying out his duties. Perhaps this was his way of apologising for the reprimand he had given me years before. Sir Stubbs gave me his autobiography, *My Life in Masonry*, as a gift and, for each year afterwards, I received a Christmas card from Sir James, and his clock.

Free and ancient masonry consists of more than just a lodge. Membership is not complete until you have joined the Royal Arch Chapter. In the mid-sixties in London, you were not encouraged to join a chapter until you were about to become a Master. In April 1966 I took Maisie to a masonic function, theatre, and dinner in London. Our host was the secretary of my lodge and during dinner I asked him which lodge had organised the evening.

"Not a Lodge Sidney, a Chapter." He replied. By the time the evening ended I found I had completed an application form and became a Royal Arch Companion in the Province of Hertfordshire. Despite losing some years of chapter membership, my progress to the First Principles Chair in 1972 was comparatively swift.

In 1976, in the Craft, I received the honour of London Grand Rank and in the same year was the founder of two new lodges. One in Hertfordshire and one in Essex. The Hertfordshire Lodge was The High Barnet Masters Lodge No.8746 at Southgate Masonic Centre, and the Essex Lodge was Fiducial Lodge No. 8753 at the Masonic Hall, Southend on Sea. I continued to advance both in the Craft and Chapter, and in 1972 was installed as First Principal of the Broxbourne Chapter in Hertfordshire No.2353. In 1976 I was appointed Grand Standard Bearer in the Hertfordshire Provincial Grand Chapter. My progress continued thus: Promoted to Deputy Grand Director of ceremonies in 1982, then followed four more promotions culminating in my appointment in 1994 to Grand Superintendent in and over the Royal Arch Province of Hertfordshire. On June 10th, 1996, I carried out the Consecration of Prae Wood Chapter. No. 8919.

1997 saw the celebration of 200 years of Freemasonry in Hertfordshire and a book was published, *Happy Hertfordshire, 1797-1997*. I became a contributor, and on p.185 there is a picture of me in my ceremonial robes as Most Excellent Companion. As with the craft, a Grand Superintendent was appointed to rule over the Royal Arch in Hertfordshire before any chapters were consecrated and, the first in 1819 was Colonel Andrew D. O'Kelly, who in 1830 consecrated Watford Chapter No. 404. The first Chapter in the province. He remained in office until 1835 when The Marquis of Salisbury (who lived at Hatfield House) was appointed. Nine more followed before me and I became the twelfth.

I recall that when attending officially, I would be announced as Sidney EE Tuck (the EE representing my middle names; Edward Ernest). I had not requested this, but when I asked why it should not be just Sidney Tuck, I realised that including the two additional vowels, one could not help but look as though you were smiling. So they continued the practice.

Lodges in Hertfordshire started to appear in the late eighteenth century, often meeting at taverns or inns. They were the best places to meet at the time, as the Lyons Corner House was when I started. For Freemasons there are three important values that help define their path through life: Brotherly Love, Relief and Truth. These inculcate Integrity, Friendship, Respect and Charity. Freemasons are focused on building themselves as people of integrity and membership provides the structure to help achieve that goal. Freemasonry provides the common foundation for friendships between members, many of which will last for life, it brings people together irrespective of their race, religion or any other perceived differences that can divide society.

The Freemasons were originally a Christian organisation, founded by the builders and architects of cathedrals as a type of union to protect members working practices, ironic as my experience of organised unions had not been positive. I was pleased to see the organisation has grown and changed to include all religions, with the central tenant of a belief in a supreme being. There are however a number of organisations connected which are still Christian, and these are shown in the following table illustrating how I progressed through membership.

Masonic Orders Membership	Date of Admission
United Grand Lodge of England	06/12/1956
Royal Arch Chapter	14/05/1966
Mark Master Masons	26/09/1977
Royal Ark Mariners	24/04/1978
United Orders of the Temple and of Malta	20/05/1980
Knight Templar Priests	03/12/1982
Rose Croix	12/06/1987
Royal and Select Masters	30/01/1982
Order of the Silver Trowel	19/09/2009
Royal Order of Scotland	08/01/1982
Allied Masonic Degrees	23/01/1988
Red Cross of Constantine	01/11/1986
The Worshipful Society of Freemasons	07/11/1988
Societas Rosicruciana in Anglia	30/06/1995
Order of the Secret Monitor	18/05/1998
The Commemorative Order of St.Thomas of Acon	21/09/2006
Degree of Excellent Master	28/11/2016
Founder	
Four Craft Lodges	
Five Chapters	
Two Conclaves Knight Templar Priests	
One Consistory Scarlet Cord	

My lifetime had seen the growth and expansion of Freemasonry. At the beginning of 1939 there were 5763 Lodges worldwide, by the end of 1948 the Second World War had seen a great increase in the membership, and this had increased to 6809. London itself had 1585 Lodges by 1995. It was not a province, Lodges and Chapters were independent units within the confines of the Book of Constitutions. The capital did not have a Provincial Grand Master and his team, just a small office, with a small staff, could not cope. Lord Northampton became Assistant Grand Master in 1995 and he realised that London needed an administrative team.

One day in 1997 I received a telephone call from Grand Lodge requesting I attend a meeting at Great Queen Street in London. The meeting was chaired by Lord Northampton and about half a dozen other brethren like me. This meeting became the creation of London Management and would consist of 21 Chairmen over 21 groups of Lodges, all having their own name. On the way to the tube afterwards, we discussed what term was appropriate to address Lord Northampton, I'd invited him to the Southgate Masonic Centre, and decided to ask him then.

"I know all your names." He replied, "You are Sidney, so just call me Spenney." That was how it was. Eventually our 21 Chairmen were found, and every so often we would all meet with Spenney and have lunch, usually at a local restaurant to discuss details for the future. I was a senior member of the Board of Directors at Southgate and was appointed Chairman of our group. As our premises had formerly been a church hall in the Chandos District of Southgate, we were named the Chandos Group. We enjoyed those years. Once a year we would hold a dinner and invite our wives, to show our appreciation at the time we had spent away from home occupied with Masonic Business, and finally, along with Lord and Lady Northampton, the Chairmen and their ladies celebrated with a dinner at The Ritz.

The Chandos Group consisted of 63 Lodges and 33 Chapters. I appointed a further 28 Grand Officers as visiting officers, who carried out their tasks well, as did the other groups. This meant that in May 2003, Grand Lodge created the 'Metropolitan Grand Lodge of London' and all the groups were disbanded.

As I progressed up the structure of the Freemasonry, I encouraged a relaxation of formality in terms of address and an equanimity in members. I believed the Masons should be egalitarian, I started changing the system from an orders and officious nature within our Lodge, to one of equality and opportunity. A few weeks after I had joined the Broxbourne Chapter I met the then Grand Superintendent of the Hertfordshire Province at a meeting. I told him I was pleased to see him again, as he must be a member of my Chapter been at the last meeting. He replied.

"My dear boy, I am a member of every Chapter in the Province, as I am the Grand Superintendent." I was humbled to have spoken to him and when I made my apologies for approaching him unannounced, he dismissed them and said, "You can come and talk to me at any time Sidney, I'm a companion like you."

The fraternal aspect of the organisation meant that colleagues became like family, and indeed, I felt like I had two families during that period. You can choose your Brothers and Companions within a Lodge or Chapter, but you can't choose your family. I was as busy with one as the other.

Receiving the Honor of Active Grand Rank at The Grand Lodge, Queen Street, London (1982)

Grand Superintendent (1995)

Masonic Ladies Night, Myself and Maisie

7

DIFFICULT TIMES

I was drawn to some other ceremonial organisations, and the nature and structure of their work, perhaps because of their familiarity with the community of the church at St. Pauls where, until marriage I had been a regular attendee. I became a member of The Rotary Club at Finchley in the early 1970s, invited by two friends of mine, Arnold Lever (a local JP) and Eric Pugh, who was my solicitor. It was a club with a long history, formed in 1926 by W. Ramsey, an Australian who was one of the founders of Kiwi shoe polish. The club thrived, with well over 50 members, which included most of the executive of the Borough of Barnet Council. I progressed through the ranks, as I had with the Masons, and became President in 1979. During that year we formed a new Probus club, and twenty-five years later, they invited me back to speak to them. My speech lasted exactly 25 minutes. "Just right." They said.

As local government officials were members of the Rotary, it was a good place for networking and gaining clients for the jewellery business and for philanthropy and charitable causes. Every Sunday in the summer we would drive the needy and the elderly out to the Hertfordshire villages for coffee and an outing. We'd take trips to London too, to Hyde Park, and past Westminster. As I was driving one old lady in her eighties past Buckingham Palace, she suddenly piped up. "I've never been to London." She'd lived in Finchley, less than ten miles away all her life and never taken a bus or a train.

We had one Rotary club member who was a bank manager. When he died, he left a considerable sum, into four figures, for charity. He made a request in his will that I be the one who should run the committee to handle dealing with his legacy. I was asked to arrange speakers for functions too, and on one occasion, sourced a character who seemed interesting, and was the Mayor of London at the time, Ken Livingstone. He approached me after lunch to ask for his payment, but I couldn't give it to him. "You want the money for a boys club in Willesden, but we can only give funds to recipients in Barnet." I said. I don't think he ever forgave me for that, although we did give him a small amount from club funds in the end.

In 1974 I had a phone call from a customer who lived in New Greens, a semi-rural area to the north of St Albans. He was a butcher and was retiring and wanted to buy or sell some sovereigns. Like many of our clients, he didn't want to come to the shop for this task. While we were chatting in his house, he received a phone call and stepped into the other room to take it. "I apologise for the interruption." He said. "That was bad news, it was the estate agent, I was wanting to retire to Norfolk, but the sale of my house has just fallen through." It was a lovely house directly opposite the playing fields of St. Albans Girls' Grammar at the front and open fields at the back. After a moment's thought, I grasped the nettle. I asked how much he wanted for the house. My impertinence was timely, I ended up buying subject to contract. It sounds simple, but I had to sell Evelyn Avenue and raise a mortgage, so it was another year before we could move in to Sandridgebury Lane, The garden was a third of an acre and I made sure I put aside one day a week purely for gardening.

I had gone down to just the one jewellery shop in Stevenage and had five years with Maisie in our house before she became ill. We had some memorable holidays during that time. As Maisie had relatives in Canada, we visited them. We were both committed to so many organisations. Maisie joined the inner wheel at the same time as I joined the Rotary Club and, like me, she progressed through various offices, becoming their president in 1977. Our friends Paul and Joan were members with us, and we had a busy social life with them and other members. She was a strong supporter of the Mother's Union, which she had first joined at a church near Brondesbury Road where we had our first flat. She moved her membership to Holy Innocents in Kingsbury when we moved and kept her connections with them, even when we moved away to St. Albans, as she had her own car by then. By the time the Rotary Club reached the 50th anniversary in 1978 it was huge, there were at least sixty members, I became president in 1979. Maisie had become ill while she was president, we were both suffering at the same time.

When she was diagnosed with breast cancer in 1977, she was reluctant to go into hospital for treatment because of her Rotary commitments with the inner wheel. Maisie was always involved with one organisation or another, from being a Brown Owl with Guides in her youth, the Rotary Inner Wheel Club, Mothers Union, Kingsbury Ladies Choir, the Opera Society, and her support of my Masonic work. She was committed to helping others. Eventually, she went to the London Hospital in Whitechapel for her treatment.

So began a traumatic period in our lives, as I received a cancer diagnosis at the same time. Originally, as a member of The Masons, I was treated with Major Surgery at the Royal Masonic Hospital in West London, followed by treatment at The Hammersmith, a major teaching hospital in White City. I kept the jewellery business running while I was in hospital by asking if I could use the ward phone. The nurses would push it over for me on its trolley while I made my calls, this could take some time, and they did complain about me using the phone all the time, but they still let me.

The Royal Masonic Hospital was renowned for its clinical research and Nursing School. When the Nurses had completed their training, they were presented with a silver belt buckle in the form of the Square and Compasses, The Hospital was eventually sold, the Nurses School closed, and the buckles are now collector's items. It was the skills and knowledge of the surgeon, a Mr Riddle there, that ensured I survived. Albeit I lost a lot of weight.

Years later, I went to the doctors and when I walked in, he said. "Here's a chap who shouldn't be here, you had six weeks to live when you had cancer." Nobody had told me that, I had carried on as normal. I was incredibly lucky to survive, but I lost Maisie to the disease. Sadly, her cancer metastasised and spread to her brain, it became inoperable and she went into a coma and died in The Royal London in January 1980, leaving myself and our boys, who were in their twenties. Clive was married with two children by then, Joanne and Simon, who were still young, and it was sad that they had so little time to get to know and cherish their grandmother. The vicar said in his eulogy at her funeral;

We assume, all too readily, though naturally enough because of our deep sense of loss, that Death, by its very nature, is a disaster for those who die. Our Christian faith lends no support to this view. Indeed, it suggests that life beyond must rather be regarded as a great adventure. In such an adventure Maisie Tuck will play her part, as she always sought to do in everything she undertook. She was never a passenger, but always a participant.

Our family received over 200 cards and letters of sympathy including from the Mayor of Barnet, in addition to a gift of three trees planted in memorium in the Jerusalem Forest, Israel, from Harold and Ann Hare.

I was grateful to be able to visit the forest a short time after. I also went with Chrys after we were married, and we stayed two nights in a Greek Orthodox Church with the monks. They had a tall, stone clock tower with a clock that had not worked for some time. I said I would be happy to have a look at it for them and climbed the precarious sets of steps and ladders to the top. It was rusted, but repairable, but the parts were difficult to get hold of and when the monks offered, I could stay for a year for free to mend the clock, I declined.

Margaret Thatcher was our MP and an Honorary Member of the Rotary Club. She used to come to several of our functions and always came to the president's night where as Vice President that year I looked after herself and Dennis. He always had a joke to tell and she remembered everyone by name. In 1979, the year I was President, she became Prime Minister and could not attend for security reasons, although Maisie and I continued to enjoy other Rotary social occasions that year, including the district conference at Eastbourne.

After Maisie died, my commitment to Rotary changed. The club began to shrink, the membership had been mainly small shopkeepers and with big, out-of-town stores increasing in number, the small shops and businesses were closing. Lunch time meetings were no longer viable, and we took the decision to have our meetings in the morning and be a breakfast club.

Despite opposition over the years, the Rotary Club started to admit ladies and I found some of the new members attitudes difficult. One chap asked, "Why do you have to say grace before the meal?" and another added, "Why do you always toast the queen?" The quality of the members was changing, there was a danger of losing traditional elements, so in 2002 I resigned. The Club struggled on and eventually closed in 2010. They had a final dinner to which we were invited, and later that evening I was named a Paul Harris Fellow in appreciation of services rendered to the Rotary Foundation and presented with a Certificate.

I remained loyal to the Freemasons. I had discovered earlier on in life how attending their meetings would relieve the stresses and worries of business life. I would attend meetings and return home relaxed and rejuvenated, stress free until the next morning. So, after losing the love of my life I threw myself back into Freemasonry.

In 1982 I received the active rank of Assistant Grand Director of Ceremonies in Grand Lodge which meant a more active year accompanying visiting officers to special meetings. In 1984, I received the honour of Past Assistant Grand Director of Ceremonies in Supreme Grand Chapter, and in 1994, Grand Superintendent in and over the Province of Hertfordshire, an office I held until the age of 75 in December 2000. Finally, in 1999 Grand Lodge promoted me to Past Grand Sword Bearer.

This was not before an organisation was instrumental in my meeting my new wife. Members of Freemasonry and the Rotary gave me great support after I lost Maisie and I was out at one or the other almost every day. One member gave me details of a charity night dinner in South London and I agreed to attend. It was held at a hotel some way from home, and as I intended to try and relax and have a drink or two, I decided to book and stay the night. I meandered down for breakfast the next day, in no hurry to leave and return to an empty house. After a few years I had grown weary of not having company at home, of having no lady to go home to or take anywhere. I was lonely.

There was only one other person in the dining room, and a noisy parrot! It's chirruping's initiated a conversation between me and the stranger. The lady had been to the same dinner as me the night before and enjoyed it. We had breakfast together, and when I found she lived in Edmonton, I offered to drive her home, it was on my way.

Chryssoula and I talked en-route and when we arrived at her home, she invited me in for a cup of coffee. I took off my coat and a button almost pinged off it. Chrys picked it up. "I'll sew that button back on for you." She said. Maisie had been a dressmaker, and perhaps I always appreciated those practical and creative skills, but because of that button, Chryssoula and I exchanged numbers and so began the start of a new relationship.

This was in May 1981. A few days later I travelled to Jerusalem. I had booked a holiday with the intention of visiting the memorial forest where Maisie's tree was. I sent Chyrssoulla a card from there, and when I returned, I rang her and suggested I take her out to dinner. We got to know each other a little more. She told me she was born in Cyprus in 1933, her first husband was killed in the troubles over the partitioning of Cyprus, and she was left with a young daughter. Chryssoula worked at the air force base in Cyprus, where she met her second husband who was in the RAF. In 1962 he returned to England, bringing Chrysoulla and her daughter back with him. They were married, but it did not work out and she went on to work in the office of Zodiac Maritime in London, living in Edmonton.

I would pick Chrys up after work and when she helped at a soup kitchen for the homeless in St. Botolph's, we'd go out for a meal after. I introduced her to my family and friends, who took to her very well. Late in 1982 we became engaged and went on holiday to Greece, travelling through Istanbul and Cyprus. We were married in 1983 in St. Albans' registry office, with a blessing a week later at St. Botolph's, Aldgate and a reception in a school near the church.

I had warned Chrys I would be out a lot, through my commitments to The Freemasons and the Rotary, and things could get worse. She accepted this, she had commitments herself. After we were married, Chryssoula joined the Inner Wheel Club at Bush Hill Park and I became a friend of the Rotary Club. She progressed in the club to become their president. She also became a Lady Freemason, initiated into The Gothic Lodge no.27, where she progressed enough to be offered the chair. She declined but retained membership until she was diagnosed with dementia in 2016.

Life with Chryssoula was always going to be different to that with Maisie. Maisie and I planned to start a family early so that we could enjoy our children and grandchildren and then have time to travel the world. We had discussed the possibility of the death of either of us and agreed that the one left behind should not give up. Life was difficult alone and should we by chance meet someone else, then it would not mean that our love for each other was any less. Chrys and I moved into Sandridgebury Lane after we were married, but it felt awkward making changes to a house that had been Maisie's home and I thought it best to move. I was driving through Brookmans Park one day in 1985 when I noticed a bungalow for sale in George's Wood Road. I had a look and immediately knew that I liked it, when I took

Chrys back to see it, we decided to buy it and were there for twenty-five years, selling it on to a developer in 2006 who wanted to build flats on the site. I sold at a profit again. Good planning and providence meant I was able to sell all my properties with gains, not losses.

Chryssoula always had ideas about buying a property in Cyprus, and we were now able to do so. We visited Cyprus several times and finally decided on a bungalow just outside Paphos in a new development where we would stay at least a week every year in addition to other holidays. It has also been used by the family. We built our ties with the local community at Brookmans Park. Chrys was a part of the Greek Orthodox Church and when a church came up for sale locally, we helped raise the money to buy it, and became founders of the Greek Orthodox Church, The Twelve Apostles, in 1997.

In 1996 my organisational role increased again when I was made a Director on the board of St. Lazarus of Jerusalem. A confraternity that models itself on the traditions and ideals of the ancient, chivalric and Hospitaller Order of St. Lazarus. It is an international organisation that works today as a practical and working Hospitaller organisation, more appropriate to the humanitarian needs of the 21st century. In the United Kingdom, The Grand Priory was a British 'confraternity of hospitallers' who apply themselves to the relief of those suffering from leprosy and other diseases of the skin. It's a ceremonial, Christian organisation of ritual and flowing robes, adorned with green and gold crosses and I was invited to join and made a Knight of Grace. Like the masons, we had Grand Masters, at the time it was the Duke of Seville. It was an organisation with events and dinners I could take Chris to. When the running of the organisation moved to Paris and towards Catholicism, I and others resigned.

I was conferred another honour when I joined the Blacksmiths City Livery Company which entitled me to the Freedom of the City of London. The members of the company can vote to elect the Lord Mayor of London. I did not progress through the ranks with them as I found myself too busy with commitments to Freemasonry. I did however join the Blacksmith Masonic Lodge where I had the privilege of becoming Master in 2002 when we also celebrated the Lodge's 50th Anniversary. It was a very busy year for, in addition to my commitments in London, Hertfordshire and 20 other Provinces, I was expected to visit each of the 21 other Livery Lodges during my year of office. There were no disappointments.

Nos,

Francisco de Borbón y Escasany,

Hispalis Dux, Hispaniae Magnus

XLVIIII Princeps Magister Maximus Militaris Hospitalisque Ordinis

Sancti Lazari in Hierusalem

In Nomine Dei, Sanctae Mariae Virginis atque Sancti Lazari

per potestatem, facultates atque praerogativas Nobis Constitutionibus

tributas, condicionibus et meritis Vestris consideratis, hodie benigne

tribuimus

Illustrissimo Domino

Sidney Edward Ernest Tuck

Officer in the Companionate of Merit (OMLJ)

honoribus, gratiis privilegiisque ad eam distinctionem pertinentibus.

A Matritensi Magistrali Sede Nostra, die

XXX Mar. A. D. MMVII

Maximus Magister

GC 5215

A secretis

Cancellarius

St. Lazarus of Jerusalem Certificate

Rotary Club Civic Luncheon (1979)

Margaret Thatcher, Maisie, Myself and Dennis Thatcher at the Rotary Club (1978)

Simon's Christening (1979): Clive, Jean, Joanne, Myself, Maisie and Simon

In Memoriam

3 Trees

have been planted

in memory of

MAISIE TUCK

by

Harold & Ann Hare

JERUSALEM FOREST

JEWISH NATIONAL FUND · קרן קימת לישראל

In Memorium, Jerusalem Forest

Chrysoulla in Pink Dress, Me and Her Granddaughter, Nina at Ladies Night (1983)

George's Wood Road, Brookmans Park (1985)

8

FAMILY TIME

Siblings

My eldest sister Irene began her career as a milliner, but after she married and had children, she became a local librarian in Dulwich. Irene eloped with a London policeman who was originally from Scotland. This upset my parents, running away to get married was frowned upon in the mid-twentieth century, and sadly they cut Irene off from the family, although eventually my mother relented and went to see her. Irene moved into a council house in Dulwich, which she eventually bought through the right to buy scheme, I think it still belongs to one branch of the family. Irene went on to have five children and her youngest boy ended up at the prestigious Dulwich College, interesting because I traced an ancestor who was a teacher at Dulwich college back in the 1700s. I have also traced a few ministers in the family, including quite a famous one who was a Chaplain at Eton College.

My sister Muriel became a dressmaker and made bridesmaids dresses for our wedding and for friends. Her husband Ted was a piano tuner. She and Ted had no children, they stayed in London and later moved to Potters Bar behind the fire station.

I had a younger brother Peter who having got married, bought a house right next door to our sister and her husband. Peter was an electrical engineer, eventually he moved down to Surrey and had three children who are scattered all over the country. I do keep in touch with them all, especially the ex-wife of one of his sons, a compassionate lady who gave a kidney to her brother when he needed an operation.

My sister Vera became a shorthand typist and kept the books for a local chemist on Euston Road. She married a local London chap and they had two children. John was the milkman that Maisie met as she cycled past on her way to work in St John's Wood. Vera was widowed quite young and lived on her own for many years but then, sadly, developed Alzheimer's. She lived in Finchley, just two hundred yards from the corner shop. When she became ill, she started to wander and often ended up in that shop to buy her sherry (she was fond of sherry), uncertain how she could get home. They used to call me and ask me to go and pick her up. Vera ended up with three carers a day, one to get her up and about, one to bring lunch, and one to do dinner and get her to bed. After Muriel died, Vera moved in with Ted for a while and he looked after her.

My Boys

I used to come home from the shop and read to the boys when they went to bed. They were all different although they had the same loving environment, and I am proud of them all. Clive started reading aged three, he remembered the words on the pages I read to him, his memory was fantastic, that was his particular talent. He started school at Roe Green in Kingsbury, next door to the grammar school which later became a comprehensive. Clive went to University College London (UCL), where he got his first degree (in chemistry), then to the University of Birmingham for a Doctorate in Metallurgy. He also achieved FIMMM, FRSC and FICorr. He started his career working for Alcan Aluminium and was involved in work on developing possible battery systems for cars, including the first Sinclair electric car. He headed a team developing rechargeable lithium batteries, then in their infancy. When the company had to downsize, he had to find another job, which he did, becoming Technical Director of a company which manufactured corrosion resistant alloys. He then became Senior Specialist - Metallurgy and Corrosion for Lloyds Register and would travel all over the world, mainly to China, ensuring that the steel and other structural materials used in the construction of ships was manufactured to sufficient quality.

He met his wife through a Church at Edgware. They were both driven academically, both have PhDs and are involved with the Marine Corrosion Forum, where Jean was Secretary for 15 years. Jean's father came from Lancashire and he became Director of Social Services for the London Borough of Brent.

The love of theatre, opera, music, and performance has filtered through the generations. Clive is an Associate of the Royal College of Organists. When he worked in London for Lloyds Register, he would give an occasional organ recital at All Hallows by the Tower, a church near Tower Bridge Station and he composed music for Lloyds Register's 250th anniversary based on the hymn, *For Those in Peril on the Sea*. He's now retired and lives in a village outside Uttoxeter in Staffordshire. He and Jean do a lot of hiking and keep dogs, they show regularly at Crufts with much success. Jean is also a talented Artist with her own website and holds shows locally.

My second son Paul followed in my footsteps in becoming a horologist. When he finished training, he became involved with the people who were repairing musical boxes. He had always shown a general interest in the arts and sciences, particularly in the field of Horology. In particular he repairs, buys and sells Antique Clocks and Watches. Over the years he has handled over a thousand of these for dealers, collectors, and Museums all over the world. He is a Liveryman of the Clockmakers Company and a member of the Antiquarian Horological Society, contributing the occasional article for their journal.

He also has a collection of Piano Roll recordings, some of which are quite rare. Many videos of these vintage performances by pianists of the 1900s are to be found on his YouTube channel, RollaArtis. Many are of academic value and a few of historical importance. He knows exactly what to look for at auction and once bought a lot of old clock movements there that hadn't sold. Paul took them home to do up and sell on, one piece seemed familiar, he had seen it before at Windsor Castle. It turned out it was one piece that had been taken away from research and never returned and ended up in a box of parts at auction. Paul remembered seeing a hole in an organ at Windsor Castle and he contacted the curator. Paul was able to sell the missing piece back to the royal palaces.

The details make an interesting horological tale. The monumental organ clock was made in London by Charles Clay of Flockton around 1730 and was intended to be his masterpiece. When Clay died in 1733, it was left unfinished and his last request was that the machine should be destroyed. His widow did not allow that to happen and completed the case herself by surmounting an earlier rock crystal and enamel casket made by the Augsburg goldsmith Melchior Baumgartner in 1664. She tried to sell the finished clock in a lottery in 1740, but was unsuccessful, and at some point, it passed to the ownership of the Royal Collection at Windsor Castle, where it lay gathering dust in the basement. It was rediscovered in the late 1940s, when the architectural historian, Edward Croft Murray, and a curator at The British Museum visited Windsor. They seemed to have been given carte blanche to borrow items for research purposes. Croft Murray was a hoarder and inveterate magpie. He took the striking clock movement and dial from Clay's organ clock, and it was never returned. When he died in 1980, his collection was sold at auction at Bonhams. It didn't sell, so the auctioneer put it on his stall at Portobello market, where Paul found it, but did not think much of it, until a Portobello Road dealer he knew bought it and suggested Paul might be the best person to repair and sell it on. It sat on a shelf in Paul's workshop for a time, until a clockmaker friend visited and spotted it. By sheer coincidence, this friend later bumped into Peter Ashworth, curator at Windsor, and mentioned the movement in Paul's workshop. Ashworth visited Paul, taking with him a rubbing from the Clay clock, which exactly matched the seatboard. After some negotiation, Paul sold the movement back to The Royal Collection and the restored clock now sits on display in Windsor Castle. A story of being in the right place at the right time!

Paul joined the Clockmakers Livery Company and like me, gained freedom of the City of London. Paul has never married.

Our son Martin was our final try for a daughter, but we got another boy. He's six years younger than Paul and his birthday is the same day as D Day, June 6th, although twenty years later in 1960. When Martin got his apprenticeship, he was recommended by the head of Imperial College at the University of London to be apprenticed to the then newly formed British Aerospace Corporation based in Hatfield, Hertfordshire. He did well there and would always wear a suit and tie, as both I and my father did for work each day. His first job after after his apprenticeship was in Sales and Marketing which involved quite a bit of worldwide travel, he even got to fly on the Concorde from New York to London, where he was given a special souvenir folder to keep from the flight. In 1995, British Aerospace sold their Hawker business jet to an American company based in Wichita, Kansas. Martin was offered a position there and he moved to the USA. He's still working and travelling, lately to Australia and New Zealand. In September 1999 Martin took a plane he had been building for 5 years on its first flight from Augusta Airport near Wichita. It was a Europa kit plane N152MT. A co-worker who witnessed the first flight said, had it been anybody else, they would have been worried, but they trusted Martin's meticulous attention to detail. He reported in the company's newsletter, there was a "bit of a bounce, bit of yaw, straighten up, a bit squirrely as I tipped from one outrigger to the other, but it stayed put as I landed."

Martin met a girl from Leavenworth, Kansas and they married in 2000. Her parents wrote me a letter to tell me they were pleased she was marrying Martin. The family have a German and Swedish heritage and belong to the Lutheran Church. Martin made sure to ask her father for Christine's hand in marriage before he proposed.

I once flew with Martin in a two-seat airplane. Attitudes to flying in America are more relaxed than here, there are huge distances to cover, and flying is the quickest way. It's almost like taking a taxi, there are small and numerous airfields where there are few restrictions and formalities to take a plane up, Martin's company has its own airfield which he uses, he works as a Technical Sales Manager for the Hawker Beechcraft Corporation.

The Grandchildren

Martin has two children, Elizabeth Maisie, and Amanda. Elizabeth is the eldest, and at 18 she is starting college at Wichita State University, having recently graduated from the Trinity Academy, a private Christian school. I could not be there because of Covid 19, but I stayed up late and watched the live stream of the ceremony on Zoom. Amanda just passed her driving test, at 15. Both girls are great sportswomen, and experts in their game of volleyball.

Clive has a daughter and a son. Joanne went to Norwich University and gained a PhD in Ecology. She met a Norwegian at Norwich, Torbjørn Haugaasen. He comes from a large family and his father is a Clergyman. Joanne and Tor did their PhDs together and then went to a remote area of the Amazon Rainforest and spent an exciting two years there researching Brazil nuts and their growth methods. They discovered how to maintain sustainable populations of the tree, which can only successfully produce nuts in the wild. One day I had a call from my granddaughter shortly after she had returned from the Amazon jungle.

"Can I come and see you?" she asked. She had arrived in the UK and made it to my house. "I thought I'd tell you that Tor and I are getting married." She announced. I was pleased.

Joanne and Tor, who is now a Professor, live in Norway with their two children, Thomas and Andreas. Joanne teaches English and Biology. Thomas was the first son in the Tuck family to be called Thomas since 1704. I speak to my great grandsons Thomas and Andreas, via Skype every Wednesday afternoon at 4pm. Andreas started school last year and just showed me the new tadpoles they have in their garden. Clive was planning to visit them in Norway, but it has proved difficult in the middle of a pandemic.

Simon is Clive's other child. He went to UCL and gained a first-class degree with distinction in microbiology, but for a few years he became an actor, in theatre and playing the trumpet in some adverts. Actors have their own Masonic Lodge, The Chelsea Lodge, which I thought he might like to join but did not. He managed to buy a little house in Eastbourne, which he now rents out and got married to Natasha, who already had twins. Simon is stepfather to them, and he and Natasha had another child, Harry, and bought another house. It needed rewiring, so Simon got another degree in electrics, so he knew how to do it. Then he decided to study for a Master Mariners Certificate because he was so fond of sailing and has his own boat. He also has a part ownership of an ocean-going yacht in Greece, and every year they have two weeks visiting the Greek islands. He went back to work in the finance department at his old University where he undertakes photography for the Uni. He took a degree in photography too, Simon collects degrees like I used to collect clocks, and went on to create his own photography business, taking on wedding and commercial work, but did not continue with it as he objected people wanting to alter the photograph to make them look better.

★★★★★★★★★★★★★★ THE 146 'FLIES' IN ★★★★★★★★★★★★★★

It may come as a surprise to most of you but the 146 recently took to the air on its first flight.

We hasten to add that this 146 was only 1/30th the size of the real aircraft, is made of balsa, powered by electric motors and weighs just over 12 ounces.

Martin Tuck, a member of the Hatfield 'Comet' aero-modelling club, is a Technician Trainee in Design and currently working in Structures D.O. on both the real 146 and the A310 wing. The model was built for the 'Round the Pole' competition held at the Model Engineering Exhibition at Wembley and took Martin 150 hours to design and construct. The trickiest part of the work consisted of the double curvature on the nose and rear fuselage which was made up of thin strips of 1/32 inch balsa individually pinned and glued on each of the fuselage frames. The only visual difference between Martin's model and the real thing is two propellers on the inboard engine pods. However, these cannot be seen when the aircraft is in flight. Power to the electric motors is supplied through two wires which act as flying lines from the central pole to the starboard wing tip. Flaps and undercarriage are fixed although the elevator is trimmable.

Normally Martin concentrates on 10 or 12 foot span radio-controlled gliders but decided to make the 146 simply as an interesting project.

Martin Appearing in a Magazine

9

TIME TO LOOK FORWARD –
ALL HEAVEN AHEAD

Maisie and I had 31 incredibly happy years together, which were eventually marred by illness. Before then, in the early years, we made sure we had two weeks holiday annually. Foreign travel was not a common practice in those days, so we visited boarding houses, and, as the boys became older and more active, we hired caravans at sites beside the seaside. Our friends Audrey and Ken Cornelius had their children about the same time as us. Audrey was one of the girls Maisie worked alongside and Ken and I had started school and scouts together. He was also my proposer for Freemasonry. We would group together and rent two caravans at a site in the beautiful New Forest just outside Bournemouth. We'd hire a beach hut at Branksome Chine, spending the day on the beach, jumping waves, and digging sandcastles with the children, before retreating to the shelter of the hut for lunch with the sea spread out before us. In the evening we'd all pile back to the caravans for dinner, and after the children had been put to bed, we'd share a pleasant evening playing cards and a having a drink. There were other occasions when we would take my mother and father to Bournemouth. They stayed in a nearby bed and breakfast and spent the day with us in the beach hut.

As the children grew older and went their own way for holidays, Maisie and I started to visit Canada as she had family there, her aunt and uncle Daniels moved to Toronto after the First World War and we visited them and the CN Tower, the world's largest free standing structure at the time. We also took The Rocky Mountaineer across country, enjoying the spectacular views of Canada's wide-open spaces. We visited Vancouver which felt like our familiar city, London. In fact, we stayed in a hotel that might have been modelled on The Houses of Parliament. Every day at 4pm the American tourists queued across the lobby to enjoy a 'British Afternoon Tea'. I recently uncovered 24 reels of cinefilm of our holidays in Canada and other places. I'm unsure how I'm in the films, as I was sure I was the one filming them!

After I retired, and Chrys and I were married, we continued to travel as much as we were able with one holiday abroad every year. One of our best holidays was a grand tour of India where we stayed in hotels that were former palaces across Rajasthan. I have video cassettes of that trip, and the other countries we visited on organised tours with Saga and Thomas Cook. While we were in India, Chrys was determined to eat native, so when we came across a street café in a marketplace, she wanted to try the food. I was sceptical, I'd spotted the staff and customers picking their plates out of a street side bathtub full of dirty washing up water. Unsurprisingly, Chrys was ill the following day!

I visited Israel several times and attended meetings at Freemasons lodges in Tel Aviv where the Grand Master was Arabic and most of the brothers were Jewish. The region was in the centre of a constant conflict, but the lodges were a haven of peace. When the Arabic and Jewish brothers stepped through the doors it was as if an unwritten ceasefire had been called. Sadly, as soon as they stepped out of the doors the fighting would begin again. If only all politicians were Freemasons, although some are, wars would not happen.

In 1988 I took the decision to retire. I was 62, and could have gone on longer, but it felt like the right time to leave. By then I had just the one shop in Stevenage and stock was slow to sell. Our jewellery and high-end watches were highly priced for the local population. Stevenage was a socialist town with a lot of social housing. The government of the time had found that the socialist dream town was not really working and decided to end the public ownership so we local leaseholders formed a company enabling us to keep trading. In effect, the company bought the town so private development could happen alongside the public. I bought the freehold of my shop, but I kept getting good offers to buy it. Eventually I got an offer so good, I could not turn it down and the shop was bought by an estate agent. I sold off the freehold and the stock and the little that was left I have been selling bits on eBay over the years, some for scrap too as the price of gold improved and held. When I rang the Bank Manager to tell him of my retirement he laughed.

"Do you mean to tell me that we are going to revert to the original arrangement when you first came to us?"

"What do you mean?" I said.

"You were to bank with us!" he replied. He always had a good sense of humour. A few years ago, I had occasion to visit Stevenage and called in to my old shop which is now an Estate Agents. I stepped in and announced.

"I have not come to buy, merely to see what the shop is now like." A lady's voice piped up from behind.

"Oh Mr. Tuck, the best Governor I ever had!"

Retirement after a long life of work can be hard. One day you are one of the most important people in the district, the next day that importance has evaporated. The Borough Treasurer of Barnet was also a member of my Rotary Club and I had seen him retire and be at a loss as to what to do with himself. Bill developed a school to train people for living such a different life of no responsibility. He died a year later, and I was determined that would not happen to me. I resolved to remain active and did so through my community connections and Freemasonry. I took up golf when I was 69, although I must have a break from playing during lockdown and am not sure what condition my swing will be in when I am able to return.

Chrysoulla and I moved to Moran Close on the edge of Bricket Wood in 2006. We have enjoyed a pleasant life there, and Chrys has a live-in carer to help with her dementia. Chryssoula had one daughter named Elita, two grandsons, Phivos and Stephan. and one Granddaughter, Katerina. They used to visit fairly regularly with their own children, and she would often give them gifts of money. However, the visits have stopped since her dementia has taken hold. It is over two years since we saw or heard from Stephan, who has two children. Phivos is not married, he had a partner, but they broke up and he has no children.

He used to visit at least once a month. He was always a little closer to his grandmother having lived with us for the duration of his time at Secondary school. He is a sound engineer, mainly working at night clubs and since the breakout of Covid 19 has gone to live with his adopted grandfather (Chryssoula's second husband) as his carer. Nina has two children, Olivia and Anastasia, who are both at School. She still comes every week or so, often with the children. We often used to be invited to Sunday evening dinner, however the pandemic has stopped this for a bit. Nina seems to have a different set of values as she was brought up by her other grandmother, who appeared to be quite strict.

Chrys's daughter had veered off the rails somewhat when she was younger. I think the tragic death of her father at such an early age was something she never really got over. She could never hold a job for long and told me more than once that "only the stupid work." She wanted to buy a house in Cyprus, where her mother's side of the family originated and Chrys gave her some money, but it was less than a year before the house was repossessed and her daughter came back to England. She lived with us for a while, but we had a difficult relationship and she moved on quite quickly. She sadly died quite young and Chrys would always be upset when her name was mentioned but, somewhat mercifully, since the Dementia has progressed, she has gone from Chryssoula's memory.

I have been part of three close and complex families in my life. My own with my beloved parents, matriarchal mother and siblings, Maisie's, with a patriarchal father and similar upbringing to my own, and Chrys's fractured unit. Our family tree grows and spreads its branches as time goes by. Family is important to set values and morals, but you can make your own way in life, as I have done.

Industry and activity are part of my secret of longevity and life after retirement. I kept outside interests when I worked that continued when I retired. I took up golf for exercise, cycled and walked a lot when I was younger, now I have a static bike in the dining room and do a little each day. I have many activities to keep the mind active, and stay in regular communication with family, using remote video calls, and meeting up when we can., but must admit to being a great deal slower mentally.

I have an interest in reading theology and retain an interest in horology. I keep some clocks at home, but rarely work on them now. I have a skeleton clock under a glass dome showing the internal workings, and an ornate French mantel clock, and a striking wall clock in the hall which was the retirement gift to Chrysoulla on her leaving Zodiac Maritime. I have had many others over time, which I have now sold, many I would repair and sell on if they did not fit in the house.

A life is a fleeting moment in eternal time. When I read through the transcripts of old lectures and speeches I gave to Rotary and the Freemason's, it does not seem like I wrote them. The person who delivered erudite words to an appreciative audience had an expertise and knowledge that seems to have evaporated, I feel I have unsurpassed it since. This book forms an attempt to pass on not only my personal history, but some sense of who I am, before I evaporate into the mists of time. I will leave the last words to Maisie in a poem she composed in 1946. She would like that.

I am so sure of immortality
So certain that our lives go on and on
That the strange silence known to us as death
Is but the glad beginning, but the dawn
Of a day so brilliant
That our earth-tired eyes
Holden so long, will need a moment's space
To grow accustomed to the blinding light
Before we meet our maker face to face

And then all Heaven ahead, all sorrows past
All pain forgotten, and no need of tears
There will be blessed hours of endless joy
With God himself our comrade through the years
And he will give the work we love the best
And each to what he was meant to be
Craftsmen or scholar, moving ever up
The glittering highroads of eternity
Goodnight my sweetheart
My dearest of all dears.

— Maisie Tuck

Chrysoulla and I, Cutting the Cake at our Wedding (1983)

Outside of St. Botolph's

The Whole Family Outside the Reception

Mum's (Ivy) 100th Birthday

END OF AN ERA

IT'S THE END of an era this Saturday when Sidney Tuck, Watchmaker and Jeweller, shuts up shop for the last time.

For S Tuck, Jeweller, was one of the first shops to open in the Market Place of Stevenage New Town over thirty years ago.

'I've seen an awful lot of changes over the years' said Mr Tuck. 'Most of the old shops have gone, and the whole emphasis seems to have moved to the other side of town.'

Although Mr Tuck has three sons, none of them wanted to take over the shop, for they have all specialised in their own particular fields. 'I wouldn't have imposed it on them' said Mr Tuck, 'although I have found joy in selling good quality jewellery.

Charities

Asked what he will do when he retired Mr Tuck, who intends to stay in the area, said

**Story by
Anne Mottershead**

that he would spend much more time with his Rotary works and various charities.

By the time Saturday comes, I hope we will have sold out. We have really massive savings on all our goods' said Mr Tuck.

His manager, Adrian Ing, told us 'Over many years' Mr Tuck has striven to provide personal and expert service. In my opinion it is the end of an era for Stevenage. The shop and the service we provide will be greatly missed, not only by the public but by the jewellery trade.

'It has been a pleasure to work for such a gentleman and I wish him a long and happy retirement.'

MEMORIAL

The 58/61 Squadrons in commemoration of

pate in the project to provide a suitable memorial.

A special invitation has been extended, by the Memorial Commit...

End of an Era – An Article on My Retirement

Chrysoulla on the Great Wall of China (2001)

2001. 7. 29

Our Holiday in China (2001)

Five Generations of Tucks

Clive, Chrys, Paul, Martin with Me at the Front Holding my Grandchildren, Simon and Joanne (1983)

Chrysoulla's Family: Phivos, Great Granddaughters, Chrys, Grandson Stephan and Nina (Left to Right)

Chrys, Paul, Martin, Christine, Clive and Myself at the American Wedding

Amanda's High School Graduation (2019)

Me with Clive's Family (2016): Joanne, Thomas, Simon, Harry, Clive, Andreas, Myself and Jean

Joanne, Tor, Thomas and Andreas

My Two Great-Grandsons in Norway, Andreas and Thomas

Four Generations at My 90th

StoryTerrace